D1328726

RETURN OF THE GIFT

Michael O'Neill

Return of the Gift

PUBLICATIONS
2018

Published by Arc Publications
Nanholme Mill, Shaw Wood Road,
Todmorden OL14 6DA, UK
www.arcpublications.co.uk

Copyright © Michael O'Neill, 2018
Copyright in the present edition © Arc Publications, 2018
Design by Tony Ward
Printed by TJ International, Padstow, Cornwall

978 1911469 46 9 (pbk)
978 1911469 47 6 (hbk)
978 1911469 48 3 (ebk)

Cover image:
VASILY KANDINSKY, Landscape with Red Spots, No. 2
(Landschaft mit roten Flecken, Nr. 2), 1913.
Oil on canvas, 117,5 x 140 cm. By permission of the
Peggy Guggenheim Collection, Venezia.
(Solomon R. Guggenheim Foundation, New York)

ACKNOWLEDGEMENTS
Acknowledgements are due to the editors
of the following publications in which
some of these poems have appeared:
*Blackbox Manifold, Eborakon, Keats-Shelley Review,
London Magazine, Poetry Salzburg Review, Prac Crit,
The Reader* and *The Wordsworth Circle.*
'Not That Only' was first printed in *Prac Crit* with a
brief essay by the author, not reproduced here, but
available via the electronic pages of the journal.

**Editor for the UK and Ireland:
John Wedgwood Clarke**

For Posy, Daniel, Melanie
and Millie,
and in memory of my mother
Margaret O'Neill
(1924-2016)

CONTENTS

DAZZLE

Dazzle when headbeam after headbeam crosses.
Cessation of laughter in the back seat.
He presses his foot down, hard, then harder. The car squeezes
through a wind tunnel charged with darkened heat

that flanks the flying metal till they come
out the other side of what had the air
of high-speed death and, mercifully, the same
is true of each too close for comfort neighbour.

And the summer hurtles on: New York apartments,
eyes 'like glass ready to smash', drugged smiles, the Doors…
I travel back this evening to that hill

between the city and the forest, pause
beside the tarmac, awaiting myself, tense
and careless, deaf to any ageing call.

PORTHMEOR BEACH

The waves could get to haunt you,
growing longer and whiter,
greener and bluer,
driven in more strongly
past the Island, chapel

exposed on the top,
or urged this side of
the spur of headland
where a path
climbs towards Zennor

and a gull or two flicker
only to swing back
across boarders
in wetsuits, flailing
a limp front crawl or if

more practised riding
foothills of surf as
people dawdle, some
looking through lenses
for kittiwake or chough

– one at least on
the track of Woolf
and her primal memories,
waves breaking, filling
the 'bowl that one fills';

others trailing the painters,
thermals, windows, jumbled
perspectives, worlds ready
to be drowned, masts
jutting their verticals…

The waves would get to haunt you,
drawing you back
to the sands and the sky,
to the blue and the green,
to the wet and whiteness

of crests you'd watch
lapsing into foam, lost
soul-essences in
quest of God knows what
past the horizon.

SCENE

The Adriatic spreads to the horizon.
Our balcony gives on to the latest dawn.
It's very early, yet a boy is up and curving
into wet sparkle from a pier-like spit.

It's well under way again, this ordinary
wonder, rotated curvature of light,
event the previous lot kept witnessing
when they were the ones who loved, who thought they
    sought...

There's a low clap from where the waves collapse,
and yet a silence can be heard.
When, as I do these days, I let them catch
up on me, inklings of a final lapse,

I set them wish-fulfillingly in such a scene,
people turning sleepily or waking up,
waters extending for miles, a boy diving,
the looker on no longer looking on.

REVERIE

I was leaning on a rail
at the bottom of steps
where two streets converge –
one heading towards
stone and sanctity,
the other towards
lecture theatres and pubs.
I was waiting and waiting
and no one showed
(the wrong day),
until I drifted off, fell
into a reverie,
'a brown study',
and seemed to slide
outside allotted
purposes as body
after body scurried,
pressed and hurried
towards the next stage.

Music began to play
beside me; a young busker
with harmonica
and guitar hummed
some Bowie, strumming
shyly at first, though deftly,
then stopped, then riffed
chords of a lost song
that took me right back – *shall I*
tell you about my life?…
no one I'd rather be,
but I just wish that I'd never –
languorous, electronic
swoops, lifts and licks

that dropped and left me
in the dismal, pure
palace-vacuum of teenage
sehnsucht, waiting for
it to unfurl, waiting.

JANUS

1

Scimitar in the January sky –
it starts again,

the moon as resurgent emblem.
'Renewal', so its tacit lunar hum

might be saying with mirthless irony,
'beckons'.
         Well, why not wax as well as wane?

2

…Scimitar in the frost-clear sky
seeming to cut its own shape stroke by stroke

until it hangs there, above
us, staring down like

a painting by a cold-eyed master-monster
who has foreseen more

than we can, without flinching, bear
to contemplate the thought of.

'Don't like the Italian poems so much'
the email growled. The nerve it tried to touch
just slumbered on, but later he'd to ask,
'Why write about Venetian scene or masque
when there is plenty enough misery
for you to shape a simile
from in the street: cemented shore
wealth's tides have ebbed from?' And, yes, the raw
faces that turn up for cutback benefits
– they drag out pity as they lower spirits.

Dante would have put it better! Yet to write
about his now, the Florentine had to fight
through throngs of shadows on the ghastly river,
exile himself from time to where forever
is the present tense. Reasons mount up why
anyone might flee towards imaginary
places, or towards a real place recast
to vindicate the restless soul at last.
Such reasons might include never belonging
to a city your being seemed to be wronging,

or finding yourself often sprawled and torn
between the living, dead and the unborn,
between the farm and hospital, north and south,
between, between… the word lies in his mouth
like a dumb stone, not like an obolus
displayed on the Stygian water-bus
that will allow him the chance, Douglas-like,
to sing of what the others never took
notice of – more like an impediment,
more like blockage, in fact, than the saving stent.

A poem's ultimate nation is Utopia.
He'd travel there sometimes through Venchimera
but would want the pull towards redesign
to be acknowledged, the way in which each line
passes the baton of its mixed intentions
to every syllable. A poem's inflections
belong to the language that we cannot speak,
speak of a day that's absent from the week,
entangle themselves with crazed artifice,
concoct a lyric draught of fire and ice.

And yet, re-reading his lines, he sees that death
is in Arcadia too, that the same breath
animates them as comes from working lungs,
that freedom is limited, that tongues
of fire descend or don't in any quarter,
that what he wanted was not escape, but a
canvas he could paint himself in and out
of with a less strong sense that inhibiting gout
had seized poetic feet.
              Ariel was lonely
but had the air to fly through. Not that only.

CANAREGGIO

An electric
        storm whitening
poles striped red yellow
                beside the dock
a shuttered whisper
             resonant in your ear
ripples reflecting
          lamps hung from
bracketed stanchions
           at the entrance of
three *rami* a young child's
               crying domestic noises
voices a man's
         and then a woman's
differently pitched
         sì sì sì the storm
flashing soundlessly
          the night passing
on either side two
           iron-wrought bridges
a whistle a concave
           buckle of lightning
but still no bang from
           the sky though now
a man on
       a blue-white plastic
craft swishes through
           the swaying canal

Ibridismo

Long waits in anterooms to the heavens
and brisk hops across Europe,
then the chiaroscuro of Puglia,
Saracens, Normans, talks on *ibridismo*.

Outside a miked, deconsecrated church,
Vespas thread Bari Vecchia,
walled maze branching and slanting…
I listen to a woman with a tortured face

who holds a cigarette between tar-
jittery fingers and waves it
in the direction of battle as
ferries crisscross the Adriatic.

Rows of tents outside the airport.
'For refugees, Kosovar', explains this stranger
who appoints himself – *grazie mille* –
my craggy guide. The city

maps on to the veins of his capable hands.
He has a maker's passion for boats
and the imbrications of Arabic culture.
Our bits of languages

begin to fit like pieces of a plate
broken by a host in ancient times
– one part for the guest – in the hope a figure
would stand on his family's threshold

some day, any day, presenting a shard.

Bari 1999 – *Durham* 2017

PRURITUS

It seemed like a homing signal
gone wrong, a sizzle of badly directed
voltage sparked off by the need
to go back, to return to the riverine city
where he was stopped for fifteen minutes or so
while traffic was held though lights

changed as an Orange Lodge parade
mounted a slow, defiant climb
up Leece Street, before turning right
across his windshield, drums, pipes, and sashes
on show, but any sense of a march fizzling
out long before the last walker and her dog.

Certainly, it was over-familiar, the itch;
it wouldn't leave him alone.
In a single weekend it attended him
across the Pennines and under
the chandeliers of the irretrievably
bygone splendours of the Adelphi Hotel.

True, there were distractions, intervals
when it could be thought almost not to be,
respectfully waiting in the background
as they chatted on below the lantern vault
of the Mersey Funnel in a place on Hope Street
or watched the river's absent-minded flow.

But to deny it was there, albeit latent,
albeit like a person careful not to
show her or his possession of the whiphand
in case that closed down another avenue,
another plot or inkling of a plot –
to do so would be nothing less than foolish.

For it existed, behind one ear, behind two, along
the rim of one ear, spreading, diffusing itself
like love on Coleridge's Pantisocratic model
to the space between his left ear and collarbone;
it was now as indisputably present
as it had once been unimaginable

– intimate alien underneath his skin.

TRIOS

1

A wake of trios,
lingering thirds,
after-omens:

three military planes
at dusk, low over
fields at Ickworth;

three flights: the latest
to brooding, shadowy,
baroque Catania;

many slogs along mainly
three motorways,
through sun, rain, dark.

2

I've taken myself back
to where I grew up,
the Mersey at the

horizon-wide
road end, endlessly
mirroring mood,

with stopovers
here and there, fells
tracking my stride,

and once at Appleby
for an afternoon where
I bought two volumes of

Arthur Symons, 'Is it
your face, is it a dream?',
(sortilege of a kind

as the stiff white pages
fell open), and a book
whose name I've forgotten.

3

Through the plane's rush, over
engine noise, between steps,
I've tried to hear advice

you might have wished,
rather urgently,
as could be your way,

to impart from
your new home
in the earth or the air.

And if, sleeping,
I hugged your phantom
once, twice, and then

three times, would your
Homer-loving father not
have glanced at you,

were you both to look on
gravely, indulgently,
not quite detachedly?

TO DO LIST

Spell out the unusual place of birth
from the tracked-down passport;

collect the certificate;
make arrangements with the ceremonious

lodge (need the green form);
ring the Register Office

(entrance by the shopping centre side);
leave a message in an everyday voice

on the vicar's answering machine;
book the Church Hall;

proofread the order of service –
should 'forevermore' be 'for evermore'?

Take cards with their unique numbers
to the bank; get used

to 'sorry for your loss'; contact
pension providers; cut out the top

right-hand corner of the passport;
ask for it to be returned; dream

of her return as a young woman; live
with the images; dream

the windswept, out-of-body dreams;
scrape words together for the tribute;

say the wrong thing over and over;
start each phrase with a concessionary tic;

compulsively photograph documents;
locate the will; order

the platters of food; lug in the bottles;
gaze at her face in the chapel of rest;

wonder whether her diaphragm lifted,
whether she breathed just once.

LANDSCAPE WITH RED SPOTS, No. 2
(Peggy Guggenheim Collection)

It cuts its course, our packed traghetto,
across the Grand Canal.
                              It'd cut its course,
your death, your quick, aortic death, across
the year, as though you'd somewhere new to go.

And yet I'd keep you for a short duration,
make-believe this room bequeathed by Peggy G,
shrine to the lilt and shimmer of Kandinsky,
held essences like yours through art's creation.

Spiritual yellow arcs, halos round red spots,
leave space for spidery hints that shape
a cemetery's outline – dark tints the clue.

But 'essences like yours'… the phrase rots;
even if your features crop up
everywhere, these brushstrokes can't recall you.

CHAPEL

The stiffened limbs,
the body from which breath is gone,

the old myth of the soul,
Psyche broaching her wings –

the anima, beautiful lie
that must be true...

Waking at four,
jaw locked for no reason,

the chapel of rest awaiting you,
the candles, the good book

open at a ponderable verse,
you left alone, you, the spruced wood

and the stiffened limbs,
the body from which breath is gone.

POSTCARD

for Lee

Over a field of sunflowers
    close to the Gorge of the Ardêche
a butterfly quivers.

    The camp-site's sky's a burnt turquoise.
From all round Europe, cars reflect
    a glare rising by degrees.

It defeats me to imagine
    or believe the continued fact
you've slipped away and gone

    – you with whom I associate
child-care, Jung and gites in the Loire.
    Had we fetched up here, might

you not have made out in the loop
    traced by the spectral butterfly
the soul's dreamed-of escape?

CARE

1

Dropping by, no announcement, I come upon you,
in extremis, struggling to cope...
You greet me with a calm, insouciant gaze
as though this turn was plotted all along.
Sorted, you contemplate a summer moon
whose huge eye hangs over Garston Docks.

I fume about the carers – where are they?
You say, it's been around since Genesis,
that ball in the sky. 'I'm starting to feel the same.'
You laugh, pleased I turned up when I did,
and give me a shrewd, blue, innocent stare
that in your nineties makes
you young and ancient all at once,
then recommence your trek through space and time.

2

Clopidogrel, the drug
he won't take, that surgical man,
my father, 91; what shall we do
with it asks the shaken youth,
his carer. Put it in the bin says my dad.

Clopidogrel I mutter to
myself walking out after
helping put my dad
to bed, offering a small
gift of iced water in a flask.

'Doggerel clopidogrel dogs
my dogged steps' is my new
cheerless tongue-twister
as an oystercatcher shrills
and peeps from the foreshore,

and a plane, tilting, ascends
invisible escalators of air,
lifting my gaze beyond this place
of care, the river darker than Styx
this February, this instant

hardly plucked from oblivion.

3

I've belted back to meet the new carers;
you see them trooping up the drive and groan
at blue uniforms and bossy strides.
I laugh and beg great sire you will receive
your latest subjects with due condescension.

Your smile has more than an edge of a glint but
you acquiesce in signatures and Liverpudlian,
well-intentioned banter. The river
ripples I imagine at the end of the road.
There's plenty of time to get things sorted.

I drive home across the Pennines, dodging
shadows and lights, detours and night closures,
my own sad, stupid drama starting up,
a camera down the gullet soon,
a diagnosis and a fate to cope with.

But for the moment freedom of a kind,
freedom to speed past traffic cones and lorries
lumbering up the long inclines while headlamps
duel through the pixellated mist and ending
seems a process one could almost get to like.

REVISITING

1

It stays intact, the house I often still revisit.
There's the piano that a sister played,
the 'Moonlight', chords for my adolescent soul.
And good to see the boiler room surviving the overhaul,
retaining traces of our 60s childhood,
with its ghosts of washing on the pulley-thing
she seemed to be squeakily lowering and raising
forever, our mother, who has finally gone.

But much remains! The very shape of rooms
that seemed to cradle lives as they passed by
one another with flickers of consanguinity –
a place from which one might set out
only to find oneself drawn back,
the house I dream of and revisit here.

2

Was it the house they had before they spoke
about doing up or moving on from
some house they thought they once owned? Was it some
other place that he remembered? What was

it, if not a bad, retrospective joke,
this pull back to a room or a place
he may have lived in once and couldn't face
again, a spectral sham of a house

with an attic where, in the small hours, he woke
once and tried to hear breathing from a room downstairs
but couldn't and looked at the stilled flares
of the river lights and said out loud hades?

SHOW

in memory of Dennis Kay

I was a near-blind inside centre,
who, as our coach phrased it
in one of his kinder
match-reports – reports that we'd ponder
at break like authors scanning
reviews – depended on 'radar.'

You mastered, brain and brawn each other's foil,
the grim arts of the tight-head prop,
boring into neck and shoulder like a bull
with a subtle game-plan.
Others huddled on the touchline
of the pitch of your unstoppable

career, your near-Marlovian ascent.
You'd mimic, disarm, and reinvent
in the same breath – able at school
to convulse with laughter a Christian Brother
(so-called), strap in hand; your wit, not to
mention weight, unmanned the hardest Scouser.

We never quarrelled, but we lost
each other, closest, strangest of friends.
I acted *Hamlet* in your bedroom,
'What art thou that usurp'st…?,' discussed
each game's nuances with you on the bus home.
Legend has it you lectured once in armour.

The many intonations that you were!
Hard not to stare, then shrug, then grin
at the show you sustained.
                                    Sustain me here,
as the night-ferry navigates fog.

Sustain me – sleepless, radar down and no
melodious tears, but summoning a joke

we shared, drawn from when you asked
that long-winded interrogator
at a chilly public speaking event
(we'd already bombed) to 'crystallise
his question into a more cogent
form,' your words a mantra for us thereafter…

I try to crystallise my thoughts of you,
a drop or three of wine spilt in the fugitive
twinge of a hope
your ghost will turn up,
rally spirits, analyse how it worked,
that backs and forwards missed-man move.

MAZE

in memory of Jonathan Wordsworth

Re-reading *Borders of Vision*, I'm led
to try to re-thread
– my spur a conversational phrase –
the airy maze

of our chat about poetry.
Fishing for an opening, you might say,
'Puzzled by your love of Shelley;
still, he's an artist'; off we

would go, as you'd recite despair-
quelling lines that had made you dare
to test your daily irony, to draw light
from where it hid, and fight,

as you did, for what would lift the soul
beyond ruins whose bells no longer toll
towards a chasm or rift
where mists and mountains lodge their gift.

THE TRICK

I walk down the hospital corridor,
push open a portholed door
and watch the beds and the sick
pile up backwards into a light that more
than does the trick, the resurrecting trick.

I'm surprised at the calm
with which I'm able to welcome
figures who've gone before,
through whom a life starts to stream
as when one engages you to enquire.

'Unwisely old,' she says with the jokiness
you loved in her. 'Your soul is a chaos.
What happened to the boy who rose
early to serve at Mass,
to whom I showed, in my missal, those

photos of a friend, long gone, jaunty-hatted?
You look strange, with hair stranded
and white as though you'd witnessed a thing so bad
you'd had to repress it, and had pretended
nothing had changed, that you were glad.'

A flicker of a smile and she left me,
rehoused in the sphere of her own infinity.
Others nodded agreement with her.
Wasn't that an ex-colleague who intoned: 'We
view with sardonic pity your labour.

Time to cease self-conflict, time to accept
forces beyond you have leapt
into the ascendant. Think of your day as finished'?
I thanked him, though might have wept,
less to find myself diminished,

than to sense those souls swoop off,
borne on tides of light and dark above
the bed I'd been dreaming in and rose from,
ready to begin again, to leave
my dead behind, to know they'll call me home.

FANTASIA

Enter the lit fantasia of the day,
a gold November morning at the station.

Expel the gross realities you've lived through,
the bad dream, worry, motions of the heart.

Embark upon a start, a lithe beginning,
as though you're not that person whom you are.

The train arrives to carry you elsewhere.
It's not too late to seek a stranger life

appears to be the burden of its coming,
attended by much straightening of spines.

Time trundles through its phases while the sun
rises and rises like a brandished sword,

or like a medal in the winter sky,
or like a brilliant vacancy of light.

You feel you ought to notice who gets off
and on, and how the landscape may have changed

across the decades you've encountered it.
But these are matters you can't be bothered with,

caught in the rhythm of your destined journey.
Shadows flow past the carriage as hours fly,

and now you're in that city where you lived
after a fashion in your youth,

the city where the coffins shape themselves.
Steps past a window stumble on

a secret glimpsed and then forgotten for
eternity, although, walking out late,

you feel the old incursions of a place
that wants to shake your hand or not while night

spins back again and yields its chilled embrace.

VALUES

Values that you didn't know you held
– 'no, no', you bite back, 'not diversity,
just courtesy'… All gone, failed –

all gone, the culture of it, how we were and what it was,
toughness, endurance, a way of making jokes, and now
you're being patronised by someone young who has

only the best of motives and even smiles
uncertainly back, knowing you're a bit odd, a bit
maverick, good in doses that are very small;

'and actually you know you were the only person
who encouraged them to speak' – as though that was
a proof of anything but being vaguely human,

as though the stuff that was passed down to you
was without value and you had to relearn
tolerance, a shifting way of being true.

VARIATIONS

'A land of men and women too'
                    BLAKE, 'The Mental Traveller'

She with her middle age and sidelong wit;
he with his youth and mane and curving smile;
he with his greying hair and tired, wan smile;
she with her youth and sidelong wit.

He with his wan ideals and greying wit;
she with her young, fine eyes and washed-out smile;
she with her ageing lines and ready smile;
he with his young man's cheekbones and dry wit.

He with no sense she might be meant for him;
she with no sense he might be meant for her;
she with a brief feeling, once when he spoke to her;
he with a small pang one time she left him.

She with many years ahead; not so for him;
he with his youth, while it's mid-life fears for her;
he closer to oblivion than to her;
she puzzled by and then forgetting him.

ECHOES

Some kind of energy's gone
you think, sheltered from the heat
as the Grand Harbour bakes in its own limelight
like a celebrity who has had to earn
her aura the hard way, the way of stone.

Five Japanese women circle the next table,
order one tea and four cans of Cisk.
They're having fun. The waiter's new task
is to click the group photo. The group smile
flung into the air refuses to fall.

You recall being once not far away at night,
chanting manic syllables over and over,
crying through the dark like a baffled quester,
head full of 'ought' and 'fought' and 'sought',
cranes stilled, the creeks lonelier than a thought.

The creeks, the Three Cities, the bastions,
and, behind, Saint Publius with its bell-towers,
dive-bombed, rebuilt, named after Malta's
first saint, the man whose father Paul laid hands
on and cured – the arrangement imprints

itself on you again, even if some force
has gone and the sun is going
to burn down to this smudge of yellow
at which you gaze, still hearing the noise
you were driven to utter, its stranded echoes.

FIRST LIGHT

in memory of Chris Brooks

I wake up,
thinking *what's it about,*
his slipping off like that,
without a bit more notice?

You'd been sent home,
were meant to recover,
to rest and get better,
not be struck dumb,

not you. Instead, further
evenings of debate and laughter,
with a Scotch or two to tide us over
departure seemed in order.

Neighbours years back, for a while
we were close-ish, especially when
the *comédie humaine*
drew out your drawled smile ...

I open the shutters.
Morning cranks up again;
vaporetti stop, then re-churn
a few *calli* away and birds

fly low beyond the restaurant
where we ate last night,
watching the plane-crossed sunset
grow dragonish and wan,

as your laid-back
urbanity, grace
and riddling loss
engulfed our talk.

45

STALKER

'Cease and desist' more or less worked,
though malignancy still lurked
on the net, in the latest
misspelt post.

In the end, it's all grist;
the episode taught him one lesson,
giving, as it did, the lie
to those who deny
there is a place called purgatory,

but, were they to reply,
'In that case,
what was your sin?',
he'd be, in this instance, at a loss,

have to fall back on 'being born'.

CALLING

Calling her at night by her maiden name,
I tried to make-believe things were the same;
tried to restore her to a time
before I was born, could walk, talk, climb;
tried to give her back her youth – that gift like light –
  calling her at night.

Sleep would come then fitfully,
with its dreams of being out at sea,
with its interval before dawn
brought back the meaning of being born.
After the hours of brightness,
  I'd call her once again at night.

TURBULENCE

1

They preen themselves, yet they conform.
They need acclaim from those they seem
to patronise, and they'll deny
acquaintance if demands prove tricky.

They cultivate admirers
in whom they glimmer as in mirrors.
Ill-fitting mask, their politesse
has, like a breached defence, its pathos.

Their calls to one another are
gulls screeching over a foreshore ...
They nurse no wish to see others as
the enemy, but, should the case

dictate, their words will turn to knives,
their hatred elbow out their loves,
their shows of fellow-feeling wane,
their Janus features grow malign.

2

At least when dead, he thinks, as they rock above clouds,
buffeted to and fro by wayward upper air,
at least when dead, he won't have to think of the words
others may or may not use of him while he's here.

His rumpled flight socks can at that happy time find
their way into one of the unspooled black bags which
his going will create a need for, when his mind
will no longer sense the start of the end which each lurch

this flight over mountain and ocean makes prompts him
to contemplate. At least when he's dead he'll not brood,
he thinks, on the vanished ones he often wants to team
up with once more, to check, as he'd put it, 'that we're good'.

TWO FOR FRIENDSHIP

1 ASH-WEDNESDAY
for Michael Mack

Smudges of ash on their unlined brows,
their faces shriven and luminous,
two young women chat in the sandwich-bar;
an aura almost haloes them like fire.

Hard not to admire their pious ardour
from the space of a few feet and the vista
of decades trying not to dwell
on the fate of my religiously seared soul.

I feel a giddy ringing in my head,
but later in the day, bearing a coffee
like a gift for the gods of twilight,

here's my mercurial Jewish friend, picking up a thread
we've spun between us, rum pair jokily
redeemed by irony and anecdote.

2 ACROSTIC

for M. G.

Maybe people don't
always realise the balance, the
rare balance that has to be struck
in an editor's dealings with life, the world,
literature, but I hope
you know how much I do. Rarest of rare
nonpareils (you'll want to sharpen that redundancy!),

Giving yourself to others
all the time, holding us to
ultimate principles and the flux,
letting us learn and take notice,
leading us to look, to look for once, at the primeval, sun-
touched fell.

RETURN OF THE GIFT

His toiled-over collection –
a collector's item,
if you're a collector
of shrivelled hopes. Well,
it seems that that's what
he's become and so he
bought two affordable
copies having met someone
abroad who knew
a person who'd met someone who…

One copy arrived – fine
if a bit foxed and tatty;
then a second came from
ripoffflotsamdotcom.
He pulled open the envelope,
glanced at the cover – the best thing
about the volume,
bodies in dark
water, the flipper
foot floating –

then looked inside and read
with a mix of laughter and rage
'To X and Y with love',
two of his friends,
who appeared to have chosen,
with the prudence
of late middle age,
to detoxify shelves that held
evidence of a taint
to be sponged away, expelled.

And, behold, like a sign
that might be construed as saying
'Begone! Pitch defileth',
a note in the book, written in
his old hand, light ink fading,
flutters down on his desk,
a dead letter, vampirically reunited
with its sender, a dead self down
in the cemetery of dead
friendships, deadened and dying.

Not that his chums could have meant
this cycle to round itself out
quite so perfectly; let's believe
they weren't aware, when
sealing up 'so much ninth-rate'
poetry, moving maybe
between this house and that apartment,
that they'd contrived matters so
he would shell out loot
to buy back his own gift.

And what indeed is a gift
if it can't be politely returned,
shoved back through the teeth
of the unwanted giver, even
if he should think he'd done
something not invidious,
not inflicted himself
like a curse or a virus?
He stuck a fresh label on, wrote 'To Z
very best' with a flourish, then

airmailed it to another country.

ENDINGS

I hold my life in my hands, my first collection,
The Stripped Bed, from which I read in the upper room

of a pub that was, I'm told, a strip club
(helps to explain why that bloke in the corner...).

Line-endings tease where once a half-bared breast...
Flesh wilts before the word, crosses its legs

at tables while light ebbs over Middlesbrough,
region my father's father left for London

and the tree at whose top there was 'plenty of room'.
After I've dropped my psyche's underthings

I half-expect his dapper ghost to rise,
suggest two visits – High Force and a barber –

then tell me how the poems were at fault.
The care with which I'd listen! All's forgiven,

Grandad! Instruct me how to field these questions
I'd like to call out as I burble on.

But no one's at my side as I explore
ground-down streets. Fantasizing reception

as the wanderer who returned,
I drop into this dump of a café

with its air of a family concern,
dad broiling chips, a daughter (on the game?),

strutting across to the window to size up cars,
while the night threatens to blur or unravel...

until I'm with him in the palmhouse
(I've known it smart, then smashed, then smart again)

at Sefton Park. He snores, chin on his chest.
Soon the hazy light will coax me out

to catch the 82C and head for home,
oblivious of his panic as he wakes

among the condensation and the heat,
the aspiring, childless writhe of trunk and crown.

THE SWAN

after Baudelaire

I

Andromache, the thought of you… That river,
sad mirror once reflective of
your soul's majestic grief,
that lying Simoïs swollen by your tears,

flowed into my memory
suddenly as I crossed the new Carrousel.
The old Paris has gone (a city's shape
changes more often than the heart of a mortal).

I see what's vanished: the litter of shacks,
stacked beginnings of capitals and shafts,
weeds, blocks greened by the damp of puddles
and shopfronts' muddled bric-a-brac.

A menagerie once pitched up there.
I saw one morning, at the hour
when work stirs under bare skies and street-cleaners
raise a sooty storm in the muted air,

a swan that had got out of its cage,
dragging its webbed feet over stone
and its white plumage over rough terrain.
Beak opening near a gutter without water,

wings drawn disdainfully through the dust,
it cried, yearning for its birthplace, a lake,
'Rain, when will you pour? Thunderbolt, when will you crack?'
I see that blighted figure as a myth,

the man in Ovid, say, twisting towards the sky
writhing head and contorted neck,
twisting itself towards the ironic, blue sky,
as though it levelled reproaches against God.

II

Paris changes, but nothing about my melancholy
has shifted. New palaces, scaffolding, stone blocks,
old neighbourhoods have all turned into allegory for me,
and my memories are heavier than boulders.

An image weighed me down in front of the Louvre.
I thought of my fine swan, its crazed mime
that of an exile, absurd and sublime,
tortured by longing. And then I thought of you.

Andromache, slipped from your husband's arms,
a degraded chattel, under the thumb of Pyrrhus,
bowed in ecstasy before an empty tomb,
widow of Hector, ending up as wife of Helenus.

I thought of a black woman, skinny, consumptive,
trailing through mud and searching haggardly
for the absent palm-trees of exotic Africa
behind a huge broth of fog, a pea-souper;

of anyone who's lost what cannot be re-found
ever; of those who hydrate themselves with tears
and suck on sorrow as if it were a benign she-wolf;
of displaced orphans withering like flowers.

So an old memory sounds like a hunting horn
through the forest of my self-exile.
I think of sailors abandoned on an island,
of prisoners, of the defeated… and of many more.

PREFIX

What's in a name? I'll tell you what a name
can do for you, your stress levels, your tired heart –
it can drive you to office-rant, seem
a trick to grind your nostrils in, well... *shit*.

Let me put you in the picture. The day's
unspeakable admin has meant accessing data
on a shared file – which will not recognise
my existence, because of what I'm now a martyr

to, my apostrophe, a limbo mark
denoting grandson or descendant of,
wrecking any ability to work,
subjecting me to thoughts of what I have:

an Irish surname, good, but little
contact anymore with Ireland, just with
people who think... 'let them think their brittle
insults', I curse, mouthing another vile oath

or ten at the pissy screen, which stands
now for being written out of a language I
have no desire to speak.
                                        And the day mends
and the tribe I've come from get my

thanks for saddling me with a prefix that
buggers up this system, empire in
parvo with its codes and controlling fiat...
I switch the thing off, head out, drink some wine.

HODEGETRIA

Half-worshipping, half-spellbound, here yet again,
I see you, Madonna, as more than human,
and yet certainly as a woman,
even if you're only a vision
in tesserae, blue cubes, golden
cubes, and though not my creation,
and I'm no Pygmalion,
you're an icon I've fallen
in love with since, a young man
touring the islands, seeking shelter from the sun,
I first stood, mouth opening, before the Byzantine
sexiness of your maternal pathos;
                              then
as now to stand here, gazing at the line
that defines your drapery, at the pain
your famous tear allows us to imagine
you still feeling even in
your new transcendent condition,
is to glimpse a star whose reflection
steadies the stretch of lagoon
between Torcello and the Logos, between
trauma and benediction.

THE CORONATION OF POPPEA

Her red dress nothing but display
of what her limbs were longing for,
you had to admire the ardent way
Nero and she lit up the score

after the stage had been wiped clean
of what made eros possible:
corpses on trolleys, blood's dark stain,
Seneca facing his last trouble,

duty and honour in the mire,
contempt for any claims of reason,
protests mute in the face of threats

issued by power and desire,
any good feeling damned as treason.
You had to admire those rapturous notes.

EARTHLY PARADISE

from DANTE, *Purgatorio,* Canto 28

In the way, dancing, a woman
pivots, feet on the ground, close by each other,
   neither moving ahead of the other one,

she turned to me upon the red flowers
   and on the yellow too, with the air
of a maiden whose eyes are lowered;

and brought appeasement to my prayer,
   approaching me so closely her soft voice
was audible, its meanings clear.

Soon as she'd reached the place where grass
starts to be washed by the shining river's tide,
   she granted me the gift of her raised eyes.

   * * *

'Now since all the air must turn
in a circle driven by the primal motion,
   unless the circuit is at all broken,

the motion, striking this mountain
   as it dwells freely in the living air,
then touches into music vegetation.

And the struck forest has such power
it diffuses through the air its quality,
   essences the spinning air will scatter,

until the earth below, to the degree
　　its soil is suitable and its climate,
conceives and rears tree-rich diversity

　　If this were understood, then it
wouldn't seem strange how, without seed,
　　a plant will, in that place, take root.

You must have understood that the sacred
　　fields where you stand are full of every seed,
and yield fruits which, down there, are not picked.'

　　* * *

'Poets of old times, with their idea
　　of the golden age and its happy state,
perhaps dreamt in Parnassus of this place here.

　　Here human innocence took root;
here spring is lasting and each kind of fruit;
　　this is the nectar of which poets write.'

Then I made a right-round, total
　　turn to my poets, and saw that with a grin
they'd heard this last proposal;

　　then turned my face back to that courteous woman.

Celestia

And then they reached 'Celestia' on the boat,
and something restless stilled in call him him.
No need to make one thought off-rhyme
with something else: *leave it alone, leave it*

he heard himself half-whisper as the grinding
hello of hull and jetty started.
Water and heat combined to form a finding,
the moment one from which he'd not be parted.

And then he wondered where Torcello was,
and scanned the long horizon, searching for
cicada-haunted hints of origin.

At best, he thought, *the best is just a pause.*
At best the best of it is inner war.
The dead words are the best: love, grace and sin.

FAR

Far out at sea, the horizon
  does not so much limit as frame
our viewing; light wears on and on,
  and fails to dim.

This evening gannets hold their flight,
  then drop down through the waves,
tearing at prey that cannot fight;
  and so the ecosystem saves

itself at the cost of chilling
  collateral damage:
all that breeding and hunting and killing
  age after age.

We're part of what we look at,
  spectators on the shore who lean
towards the storm that is coming to get
  our children's children, the unborn

generations who queue in the mind's eye
  like supplicants, who're keen,
if OK with us, to hear gulls cry,
  to visit this end of the line.

NOTHING MORE

It had been nothing more
though nothing less than a soap
bubble glistening with the colour
that is exuded from the far-off air
you associate with hope.

It travelled around in its own
space, unaware that it was stirring
responses that had been forgotten
for years in those who, stuck on
terra firma, looked up, eyes blurring.

'A marvel!' they cried as the slow,
crooked ascent mocked gravity,
until cross-winds struck up and blew
it sideways and a faint 'oh no!'
rose in the throat and fell away.

BIT BY BIT

Helping that old man to his feet,
cap gripped between his teeth,
after his wheeler hit
the tarmac and he took a bath
of dirt and stone – I suppose helping him up
explained why later I felt down in the mouth.

Three of us hoisted him from his knees
to a precarious half-upright position,
signalling 'stop' to traffic that froze
as if the drivers had seen
an embodiment of what they'll come to,
a ragged heap of flesh and bone.

It was his defencelessness as he knelt
painfully that roused something close to anger
as we tried to assist, anger at what felt
like a practical joker's caper,
nature preparing one more for the end,
bit by bit, a shoe cast in the gutter.

(Figures who were lithe once
– they've moved with a stooped dignity
to being great-grandparents
in a spasm of the eye,
their youth awakened as
though a plane crossed a whitening sky.)

He said nothing, just grasped his cap,
until, wheeler righted, he hobbled off,
a risk of falling in each step,
determined to resume his shaken life,
a man who'd brought the traffic to a halt
and left a hole in the day as large as grief.

IN AN HOUR

Air traffic control will find a slot
in an hour. A cramped, ballooning hour.
A grounded foretaste of ante-purgatory.

Long enough, it seems, as dawn
flushes the horizon, to read
or even write that unfinished book.

Long enough to notice how the decades
have grown much shorter than this present
to which some destiny's consigned you,

to recall, as though you were someone else,
the many, now inevitable stations:
the glimpses, moments when you came alive,

others' quite understandable
indifference – why should they bother? –,
the kindness of those who dared

interest themselves in the spun-dry
vortex of yourself, the chances of losing
yourself in others, the missed chances.

Not that the patient captain will miss his,
now he's been radioed the all-clear.
The plane wheels round the plotted grass,

its movement a sliding behemoth's on ice,
then musters its forces and roars
towards the clouded battlements of space.

HELP

Someone stumbling ahead of us
on the trek towards check-in.
Then an upturned face, large brown eyes:
'Can you help me? Please help me.'
'I'll try. Where are you going?'
'Portugal.' 'Lisbon?' 'Yes' – not much
English after that except 'Help me please'
and words for the black metal suitcase
she struggled with. 'Hasn't it got wheels?'
'Bag is broken.' I picked it up,
asked for her boarding pass which showed
her gate opened in twenty minutes,
found astonishingly an airport helper
beside 'closing flights', got him
to take her through security.

And off she went, lopsidedly clutching
the bag with both hands. I wanted to call out,
'She's too young; anyway, the bag
is broken; please help her' – mid-teens my guess,
fluent in Portugese on her mobile,
coping in her fashion, I suppose,
perfectly well, shrewdly enlisting
the aid of a white-haired stranger
who hoped that at the flight's end
a parent or grandparent, friend or sibling
would greet this girl he'd imagined already
as a waifish daughter destined to
carry the case of herself into a future
when maybe 'help me please'
will rise up like a clue or trace
that curves towards a day when
something else occurred connected
with staring through a window
(marriage in trouble, a difficult child),
sunlight streaming like an aimless gift.

THE THOUGHT

Like Mrs Gradgrind with her pain,
he can sense it in the vicinity,
the thought that possesses his brain
more and more, as the seasons wheel

and water bubbles silverly
at his table where views spill
over the harbour and the fort;
there may be fireworks later

– yet another *festa* – and the thought
possesses him the way Syrah in glasses
with long stems rouges the times he's dined here –
20 or 30 sittings, places

neatly laid, waiters courteous as ever,
hovering, ready as ever
to joke about 'icy UK weather',
although the oldest one's not here,

a maître d' of sorts, a memory
that comes to mind because forgotten,
and the thought possesses him,
the same thought, the same

thought that wheels obsessively
like this fly bumbling round the room,
blown in by soft currents
that stir a flag in the middle distance.

HINT

I do tonight what I've not done before:
circle the outside of the Catholic cathedral
in windswept, lit-up, taxi-ridden Liverpool.
Brutalist buttresses reach from wall to floor.

Sky is a vast nowhere. Not an RC,
my mother gave the shelter of a home
to all that bore upon her – all roads lead to Rome –
and this place drew from her such empathy.

Taking in to my right the Liver Birds,
the Everyman at my feet, and the clock-tower's
red brick over my shoulder, I sense my mother's
passion for what lies to hand, voiced in words

that can't be heard. Young joggers pad behind
and overtake; her face and welcoming smile
imprint the dark but leave me full,
once more, of emptiness, mouthing without sound

what feels as useless as a prayer
breathed towards an absent
presence, in search of something like a hint
as glass, wind and stone ask 'Why *are* you here?'

BOOKSHOP

Early for my haircut with Dominic
and a good chat about the world and life,
I dipped into the bookshop, varnished stack
upon stack of words that once made me safe

against the onslaught of the minor stuff
– age, illness, death: all dull and commonplace
and yet in charge. You run and then the race
is over; you fall and find the fall is tough.

The novels that I read in avid youth –
Vanity Fair, The Castle, Middlemarch –
are ranged before me, ruins of truth.
If any vistas gleamed, arch after arch,

they've rubbed themselves out now. No chance,
no chance at all, of starting over again;
whatever they gave – some control, sure, sane
sentences shaping an intricate dance –

will have to do. And when I step outside,
I might have been away a year or so,
swimming against the sunlight's brilliant tide,
staring at nothing that I care to know.

TWO ROOMS

Yours is spacious, with, in one corner, a table
and two blue easy chairs angled
as though for a consultation.

I was less keen on the carpet mulch –
threatened one of my ocular episodes –
but the male nurse arrived, holding aloft your dinner.

You waved it away, fastidious as a dandy.
My room has an Adelphi draught (pane missing),
and a sighting of the two Cathedrals.

High-ceilinged, with a botched holy painting,
yours belongs to a grand house rising from flat lands
a few miles to the north, an establishment

run by the Augustinian Sisters of the Mercy of Jesus;
there's a small fridge beside your bed, with space
for six bottles of white wine. I've added a few.

along with other gifts: satsumas, crisps,
grapes from Chile, chocolate, a sketch-pad, crayons.
Back at the hotel my notebook's on charge

and iPhone too… I'm scribbling this
on a napkin in a place off Hope Street,
having a break from doing my bit

during your respite stint, recalling how
you looked cared-for, abandoned, gaunt, and saintly
as you eyed a crucifix, a 'great companion'.

FEBRUARY

Twilight beyond the fifteen-paned window
on the half-landing; twilight and a cold,
steady sky; you
staring at winter's outlines – spirits low

yet lifted by that air-built height,
lifted without much chance
of coming up with reasons for
embracing winter light,

there being no particular
reason to be glad trees should supplicate,
their branches stretched out so
you see through to a single star.

THE MISSIONARY

You live on, as on that slide
she showed a while before you died;
your cotton suit bleached against the fried

bazaar-congested medley of Calcutta,
the crowd's shuffling mutter
more audible now you can't utter

your tough-edged, Cork-raised bark-cough.
You're looking at a stick-thin waif
the locals want you to adopt, take off

and away, save from the mire.
Their arms windmill as they implore
you, gaunt champion of the poor.

Her eyes strain
towards me, again and again,
begging bowls brimmed by pain.

Your neck clenches, helpless with care.
You're stooping down; all I can do is stare.
The camera clicks, locking you there.

I WAS WALKING

that bit more quickly then less purposefully
down a sunlit road that ran from traffic-lights
at the town's or was it the country's edge
past fields of corn or suburbs towards a place

I thought it was my responsibility to reach,
though its coordinates or how to get to it
or where exactly I was escaped me,
walking onwards with a queasy sense

that my destination was over my shoulder,
and that that golfer, pint in hand, looked friendly,
but that his directions trailed into gibberish,
and that I'd had this feeling before,

but that this time it was less clear,
and that there was simply no shrugging off
the way precision just wouldn't preside,
or the way words wouldn't attach themselves

to places or things, or the way that light
fell like a cloudburst on a crossroads where letters
had weathered from signposts and where if asked
I doubt I could have come up with my name.

TO THE MOON

after Leopardi

A year on, I recall how
I came to this hill to gaze at you.
I was full of hurt. You hung,
as now, above that wood,
filling it with light.
But your face was clouded, shaken,
as though you wept – an effect of *my* tears,
shed for a life that had been miserable
and still is, and, in that respect, won't change,
my adorable moon. And yet it helps
to record and go over
the period of my anguish.
In youth, when hope has a long trek
ahead and memory's road is short,
there's a grace in past events, though they
were unhappy and pain persists.

HISTORY

Cordoned off one side
to find the corpse of one who'd died,
the river seemed strange again, sinister bride.

You watched it tilt its panes
in '82 while elsewhere planes
flung missiles from the Argentines.

The year before riots wrecked
Liverpool, Toxteth looted and sacked,
hatred and rubble – blocked

up now, your lost-in-Scouseland youth,
your deafness to the city's mouthy
pride in docks and salt-sea truth.

Nothing to do with you, it never
was, even when on a bridge over
the Wear buckets filled for the miners

a few years later, not your fight:
hard to know how you should have fought
when so many seemed up for a fight.

'A tale', the psalm says, 'that is told.'
The weirs still twine and twist and fold
their ropes of wet, braided and cold,

don't give a damn about you, though
you like them, like their practical no-
nonsense focus, their end-stopped go.

IN THAT CITY

the young women are pale, oval-faced,
usually fair and have thin lines
round their mouths as though
ready for kisses or disappointment.

Tiredness shows in the cavernous
pools of their mothers' eyes,
eyes that seem to hoard
secrets of a joyless struggle.

Nothing can make it right, they stop just
short of telling you, and yet
a joke has them laughing,
young again, dyed hair mere camouflage.

They recall their difficult fathers
fondly as they gaze from trams at the wide
river that curves for hundreds of miles,
then empties itself in the sea.

STATION

Above the platform
trees in tiers resume
their time of blossom.
They're staying schtum
about the wider picture.
Their sway's a blank rapture,

transfiguring the station
until, like a migraine
aura, a shimmer forms
that seems to freeze then say:
just you see;
there'll come a day

when you'll not
be able anymore to wait
for the southbound train
to pull you away
from this interlude
of green-boughed arms;

there'll come a day
when the infinite
supply, the interplay
of leaves and light
and looking (just you wait),
won't be renewed.

GERMAN CITY SONGS

1 Muenster

A small creature trundles across the midnight road.
The city, a breath held and then exhaled,
reinstalls its comforts; the stilled

bicycles are securely stowed,
their lofty, ride-me handlebars at rest.
Silence and darkness lower their cover

over the Aasee where you strolled before dinner.
Geese and rabbits tiptoed towards one another
but didn't encroach – exemplary neighbours.

Joggers plodded, lineaments of stressed
determination on face after face.
You mimed inwardly a sympathetic grimace,

not that anyone looked for sympathy.
The old town, bombed to smithereens in the War,
hosted the famous Westphalian Treaty.

It's been rebuilt. Holiday houses far to the north,
near the Baltic, promote the boosting of health.
Set for your part on detached good humour,

you feel you're taking a vacation of a kind,
walking idly yet with intent
towards a half-closed door,

as though able to leave behind
whatever it is that drives you here and there,
that only sometimes wakes you far too early.

2 Wuppertal

The Emperor's carriage
hired for a jaunt
– we swing and slide
over a matrix of roofs
in this mid-air

suspension train
roads the river
hills that seem below us
as do church spires
houses unearthed new

construction sites
city in decline
taking its migrant quota
taking its cue from Tuffy
baby elephant who fell

from the tracks a
century ago
none the worse for
that dunking that unseemly
ton-weight descent

everyone's survival
icon none the worse
for his precipitate
baptism unlike me
out on the town past 60

with gorgeously witty
Frank till far too late
plane to catch first thing
knocking back a glass
but grimly sober

CRISS-CROSS

All down the Fondamente Nova
there's a cellular dance of heat and motion.
Even the stakes eye up the skyline
where Torcello's mosaics move a

young couple, as time-plates lock,
in 1978 when they see
how the apse stores unfathomably
a tear upon the Mother of God's right cheek.

An ambulanza flashes past;
motor-boats bounce and crest.
And now two vaporetti buoyantly sustain

their rows of gazing heads and criss-cross by.
Cypressed San Michele still looks back like a destiny
deferred; blue tesserae still stitch the sky's gown.

ROMAN FOUNTAIN

after Rilke

Two basins, one rising higher than the other
out of a round, antique marble rim,
water from this higher one brimming
over into what waits below, more water,

its quiet folded within the other's tact,
and, as though a palm opened, secretly
showing the other behind dark green the sky
like an opaque object;

diffusing itself in the exquisite basin,
ring by ring, with no wish for origin,
only sometimes, in drops, dreamily

lowering itself past the fringes of moss
onto the final mirror, which makes its dish,
calmly, the end and site of process.

FROM THE CANCER DIARY

I SCOPE

'Gastroscopy catastrophe'
I mutter the ill-charm
while *Abba* and the like muffle
the call-out of each name,

so much so I shift seats
until I'm summoned by my nurse
for the procedure.
Things will be worse

than I fear when
I wait in recovery
having had sedation
because of high BP.

I'd kidded myself I might
get away with it, but
the grave gentleness
of the staff giving my result

to me, my wife, and daughter
who forces back tears
at the word 'cancer'
confirms worst fears.

'Gastroscopy catastrophe'
I mutter like a vindication
on the way out, almost reaching up
to push open the lid of a coffin.

ɪɪ Just as

in 'Sad-Eyed Lady of the Lowlands'
possibly the finest line
and your saintlike face and your ghostlike soul
runs along the nerves like wine
because of the earlier abundance
of allusions to the material

so in the course of my illness
the fact that we love to crack jokes,
to talk nonsense and pass
into a private idiom
may hint there's a hope that lurks
in the disease's very medium
which has the force of a dumb yes,
a wry, destructive, passionate kiss.

III IRONIES

The ironies
(and incidentally,
Thomas Hardy,

you're if anything
understated
in this domain),

which included
the touchingly groundless
cancer scares of others

and months spent
worrying about earache
that masked a far more

insidious illness
seemed – hard to find the right
word – seemed, let's settle for *grotesque.*

The ironies stalked
out of the shadows and
taunted him like school bullies.

iv ON HOLD

A few strides from my carriage at Kings Cross
and the line jumps out alive in front of me
goes through me like a spear of white fire
When I have fears that I may cease to be

All weekend mind the gap is in my mind
and the gap widens and widens
the gap between the swallowers cheerily
laughing and swallowing in Jack Horner's pub

and a malignant strictured foodpipe walking freely
as though it had a right to be a person

I make an excuse and leave quickly
and breathe the unsolacing bracing
Bloomsbury air while the day turns inside out

When I have fears... cease to be
Put it on hold I tell myself put it all on hold

v Wine and Roses

Outside a faint mist
in the autumn air

'They are not long, the days of wine and roses'
read from my iPhone screen

you leaning forwards
tucking strands behind your ear

absorbed in the beauty
me voicing the remaining words

like a defrocked priest '…then
closes within a dream'

vi Mists

Mists spiriting up from the fells
the sure and certain knowledge

they will continue to rise and catch
the gaze of others

after I'm no longer around
to steer the car towards

that imaginary vanishing point
I've had in mind for many years.

Or the leaves struggling free of branches
back in the old garden as every September

(it wouldn't surprise should a figure with pince-nez
turn up disconsolately pushing a pram)

girders and trucks banging out their dissonant music
from the nearby Garston container docks

my father in his chair in the Long Room,
reflecting on who knows what,

me lingering on beneath the wide sky

VII Paths

The path you trod as a boy
round Tarn Hows

The same path you trod some months ago
on the cusp of starting to get worried
preferring soup softer food

Paths you've trodden you won't tread again
paths you'll never tread

and now on the same path taking in
silence a rusty-brackened silence

still as the day you stood by your mother's grave
after the diagnosis stood by her engraved headstone

one task you managed to complete
Tarn Hows and the search for silence

What it feels like is a half-blocked drain
running down the left side of my throat
where food seems to stick though the stricture's lower.
A double gulp once helped; now it does not.

I'm not wasting away but have lost ten pounds –
I tell the GP I'm on a sub-Byronic diet
of rich tea-biscuits and sparkling water.
'Wouldn't he have had laudanum with that?'

The dieticians look at me with appraising concern,
think up ways of fattening the cancerous man-calf;
I must fortify each mouthful with cream or sauce,
keep up the protein intake, for once knife

incises or cell-destroying chemicals kick in
I'll need, I'm told, every ounce in my frame.
In hopeful moods I see a ravaged, purified self
in a lit space, answering to my name.

IX MEDICAL PHYSICS

I and my laptop are Crusoe and Friday,
the waiting room an emptied island,
serenaded by Smooth radio.

All the others have gone now –
the various older women:
one from the Dales who'd not seen the city before,

in for a thyroid scan;
one from Peterlee altogether less happy
having her bones examined;

and one who emerged from various sessions
to announce to her stoical husband
'There's nothing wrong with me.'

How I envied her that assurance,
wondered whether we could swap lives…
Two hours for the tracer to pass

through my kidneys, blood then drawn every forty minutes
from a cannula skulking in my right arm.
I no longer bother to furl my shirt sleeve

over it, head towards the 'patient toilet
(nuclear medicine patients only)'
like a newly admitted member

of a club no one wants to join.

x Those days

I couldn't think except through literature
which gave me guises, methods of response,
a way of cloaking the brute fact of cancer,
implausible, I grant, but a defence.

As if the worst had fallen which could befall
offered a form of solace at the start.
I tried to tread the lowest deep, build a wall,
set limits to the damage through a jut

of the jawline, a contra mundum pose
that played on the idea of seeming strong,
a complication lost on those
unused to illness and its frightening,

grim humour as it changes lives,
flaying all residual pride
as in some savage parable that thrives
on showing up and shaming hints of 'side'.

When Lara's gaunt heroics failed
to work, *The interim's mine… to say 'one'*
tided me over, Hamlet's becalmed, soiled
inkling before the body-heaped ruin.

That helped. You bookish critics who disdain
allusions in your nuanced fashion, 'tough!'
Bob Dylan, too, helped me keep on keeping on;
words helped, they helped a little, when the going got rough.

'Results day and a "mixed bag",
in the surgeon's words,
and not at all clear curative
rather than palliative way
forward is possible.
Villain of the piece
is the PET scan
which has found nodes
in the neck, involving
an even more hazardous
op – and much worse
a "hot spot" in my left hip,
which may be a false positive
and may be malignant.
MRI to check in a week or two.
If that's a secondary,
no op, and a dismal
prognosis. Still
no clear treatment plan.
Terrible for everyone round me.
I feel unnaturally calm,
fine really…'
                    Thought I might
have 'scaped whipping, but
from the moment he entered
it was clear there was bad news
to be dispatched which he did
with professional clarity.

I was listening
for some reference to
being healed, but that didn't
seem to be part
of the script anymore.
A sub-text perhaps.

XII SUNDAY

for Posy

When it's time sometime to find
my notes for tomorrow's lecture
which it appears after the latest deferral
I'll be able after all to offer

when according to our five-year-old granddaughter
sage delighted by her new knowledge
God rested after creating the world (so many trees!)
in his own likeness and image

when wife and husband for forty years we sit in the parkland
like carvings of sorrow almost at peace
and the medical mill ceases to turn
and for a while all seems as it was

Chilling in the kitchen, my warm,
chatty daughter humouring her wordy dad
and his immersion in long silences…
Not for the first time we're enjoying time-out
time in one another's company.

Before you went to school and I to work
we used one term to watch this daffy film.
I liked the protective father's '45 and a shovel'.
After a fortnight's sporadic viewing, I remarked,
cluelessly, 'this reminds me of an Austen novel'…

'Remember the day', I find myself
saying, 'when rain lashed Funchal
and you and I took shelter
in some dive? Neither of us spoke at all;
just did our thing.' 'Yes, *Café XX*',

you reply, flashing me a google snap
that looks like nothing I remember. 'Well,
I wrote a poem about us and that day;
it'll be on a clapped-out, useless laptop.
Wish I could find it.'

You don't seem too overwhelmed
by this loss to our literature;
we carry on just sitting here,
the lost poem slowly reviving
in one another's company,

the future seeming real once more.

BIOGRAPHICAL NOTE

MICHAEL O'NEILL was born in Aldershot in 1953 and moved to Liverpool in 1960. He read English at Exeter College, Oxford. Since 1979 he has lectured in English at Durham University, where he is a Professor of English and currently an Assistant Director of the Centre for Poetry and Poetics. He co-founded and co-edited *Poetry Durham* from 1982 to 1994. His recent critical books include, as co-author (with Madeleine Callaghan), *The Romantic Poetry Handbook*.

He received an Eric Gregory Award in 1983 for his poetry and a Cholmondeley Award for Poets in 1990. His three previous collections of poems are *The Stripped Bed* (Collins Harvill, 1990), *Wheel* (Arc, 2008), and *Gangs of Shadow* (Arc, 2014), and his poems have appeared in many journals and anthologies.

He is married with two children.